DIRTY AND DANGEROUS JOBS

Oil Spill Cleaner

By Tracey E. Dils

Reading Consultant: Susan Nations, M.Ed.,
Author/Literacy Coach/Consultant in Literacy Development

Marshall Cavendish
Benchmark
New York

Dedication: To Ella Bella Boo and Nicholas

Copyright © 2011 Marshall Cavendish Corporation

Published by Marshall Cavendish Benchmark
An imprint of Marshall Cavendish Corporation

Other Marshall Cavendish Offices:
Marshall Cavendish International (Asia) Private Limited, 1 New Industrial Road, Singapore 536196 • Marshall Cavendish International (Thailand) Co Ltd. 253 Asoke, 12th Flr, Sukhumvit 21 Road, Klongtoey Nua, Wattana, Bangkok 10110, Thailand • Marshall Cavendish (Malaysia) Sdn Bhd, Times Subang, Lot 46, Subang Hi-Tech Industrial Park, Batu Tiga, 40000 Shah Alam, Selangor Darul Ehsan, Malaysia

Marshall Cavendish is a trademark of Times Publishing Limited

All websites were available and accurate when this book was sent to press.

Library of Congress Cataloging-in-Publication Data
        Dils, Tracey E.
           Oil spill cleaner / by Tracey E. Dils.
        p. cm. — (Dirty and dangerous jobs)
        Includes index.
        ISBN 978-1-60870-174-2
        1. Oil spills—Cleanup—Vocational guidance—Juvenile literature. 2. Oil spills—
        Environmental aspects—Juvenile literature. 3. Petroleum engineers—Juvenile literature.
        4. Sanitary engineers—Juvenile literature. I. Title.
    TD196.P4D55 2011
    628.1'6833—dc22   2009049822

Developed for Marshall Cavendish Benchmark by RJF Publishing LLC (www.RJFpublishing.com)
Editor: Richard Hantula
Design: Westgraphix LLC/Tammy West
Photo Research: Edward A. Thomas
Map Illustrator: Stefan Chabluk
Index: Nila Glikin

Cover: A worker helps clean up a 2004 oil spill in the Delaware River between Pennsylvania and New Jersey.

The photographs in this book are used by permission and through the courtesy of: Cover, 4, 15: Getty Images; 5: iStockphoto; 8: © Jean Louis Atlan/Sygma/Corbis; 13, 18, 20: AP Images; 9: SCG photo by PA2 Eric Hedaa; 11: © Photoshot Holdings Ltd/Alamy; 12, 24–25: NOAA; 17, 26: AFP/Getty Images; 19: © Natalie Fobes/Science Faction/Corbis; 22: Coast Guard photo by Petty Officer Jonathan R. Cille; 28: Reuters/Landov.

Printed in Malaysia (T).
135642

CONTENTS

Words defined in the glossary are in **bold** type
the first time they appear in the text.

Oil Spill!

In this 1979 spill from an oil well in the Gulf of Mexico, some of the oil caught fire.

When a major oil spill happens, the result can be a huge disaster for living things and for the environment. Oil spill cleaners are the people who rush to the site of a spill to limit the damage. What they do is messy, sticky, stinky, and dirty work.

It is also dangerous. Oil is toxic, or poisonous. If it touches the skin, it may cause a rash, and the poison may pass through the skin into the body. Breathing in oil fumes can damage the lungs. The cleaners often work in remote areas, harsh climates, or terrible weather. Cleaning up oil spills is not easy or safe—but it is important.

Moving Oil around the World

Crude oil is used to make gasoline, jet fuel, and diesel fuel. Without these fuels, most cars, planes, trucks, ships, and trains wouldn't be able to move. Many other important products also come from oil. Plastic is made from oil. So is the asphalt that is used to pave streets. Laundry and dish-washing detergents, some medicines, and even disposable diapers are made from oil.

Crude oil is usually found deep underground. People drill wells to get it out. Most of these wells are on land. Others are in seas and oceans, where oil lies underneath the sea floor.

Most wells are far away from places where oil is used. The oil needs to be brought to these places. Every time oil is shipped, there is the risk of a spill. A big spill can be a big problem.

This pipeline carries oil all the way across Alaska.

Spills Happen

Barges and large ships called **tankers** often handle the job of carrying oil over water. Trucks and special train cars haul oil over land. Pipelines also carry oil.

The oil is handled carefully. Still, an oil spill could accidentally happen. A pipeline might leak or even break, letting oil pour out onto land or water. A truck could get into an accident and spill its load. A tanker might be caught in a severe storm at sea or might hit something—such as a **reef**, an underwater ridge of rock close to the surface of the water. Whatever the cause, the tanker might be so damaged that it spills oil into the water.

Major spills don't occur only when material is being shipped. An oil well might have a **blowout**. A blowout occurs when too much pressure builds up inside the well. The well can't control the oil, which shoots out. Today,

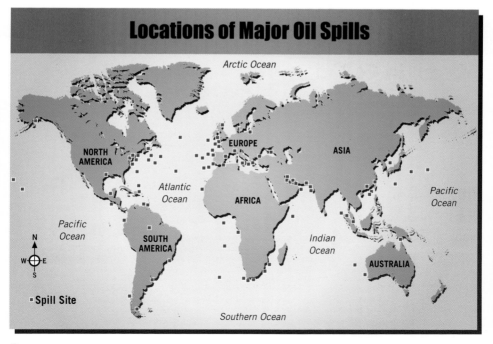

Kaboom!

If fire happens to break out on a tanker, an explosion may result. Some of the world's worst oil spills have been caused by explosions. In 1991, the tanker *ABT Summer* exploded in the Atlantic Ocean, about 900 miles (1,400 kilometers) from Africa. It carried 80 million gallons (300 million liters) of oil. Some of the oil burned, and some sank with the ship. A lot of it spilled into the ocean. Also in 1991, the tanker *Haven* exploded off the coast of Italy. It sank and continued to leak oil into the Mediterranean Sea for years. The size of the spill has been estimated at 45 million gallons (170 million liters).

because of improvements in drilling methods, blowouts are much rarer than they used to be. But they still happen.

Oil can also spill out of storage tanks. A natural disaster such as a hurricane or an earthquake may damage a tank enough to cause oil to leak out of it into the surrounding area.

Also, spills can be intentional. During a war, one nation may dump oil on purpose—and perhaps even set it on fire—in order to hurt the enemy or block the enemy from invading.

Midnight Collision

One of the worst spills in U.S. history happened just after midnight on March 24, 1989. The giant oil tanker *Exxon Valdez* had just left a port on the Alaska coast. Suddenly,

No Accident

It may be hard to believe, but the world's largest oil spill happened on purpose. In 1991, during the Persian Gulf War, the Iraqi forces wanted to slow down U.S. troops. They spilled as much as 460 million gallons (1.7 billion liters) into the Persian Gulf, and they set some of it on fire. The spill and fires did not stop the U.S. troops, but they did cause a lot of damage to the environment.

Workers try to limit the damage on the Alaska coast after the *Exxon Valdez* oil spill.

the ship hit a reef. The reef ripped a hole in the tanker. Oil gushed out. Almost 11 million gallons (42 million liters) of oil poured into the Pacific Ocean. That's enough oil to fill about 430 classrooms!

The spill occurred just a few miles out to sea. It did not take long for the oil to wash ashore, threatening plants and

Oil-Eating Bugs

There are tiny **microbes** (living things so small they can be seen only under a microscope) that "eat" oil. They break it up into simple substances. These microbes are nearly everywhere. Because of them, the oil from a spill gradually disappears. The microbes work very slowly, however. They are of little use in spills that need to be cleaned up quickly. Still, in some cases—such as when other methods cannot do the whole job—they can help in a cleanup. In these cases, workers may add **fertilizer** to the spill site to help make more microbes grow. When there are more microbes, more oil gets "eaten." To help get the job done more quickly, workers may also bring additional microbes to the site.

animals there. Strong winds made the oil move toward the shore very fast.

Blowout

The *Exxon Valdez* spill was actually much smaller than some spills that have happened outside the United States. An especially big spill resulted from the 1979 blowout of the Ixtoc I oil well in the Gulf of Mexico. This well spilled oil into the water for nearly a year. The spill totaled about 140 million gallons (530 million liters). The oil polluted the water and threatened the plant and animal life in it. The well was located far from land, however, and much of the oil gradually dispersed, or broke up, into small and relatively harmless droplets. Only a portion of the oil floated to the coast.

Oil spill cleanup is messy work.

Cleaners to the Rescue

Oil spills can kill birds, fish, and other living things. If not cleaned up, a large spill can ruin a **habitat** for years to come. Oil can also enter sources of drinking water. That can cause serious health problems for human beings. When a spill poses a serious threat to people's health or to the environment, help has to come quickly. Starting cleanup promptly is particularly important for spills on water. Since oil is lighter than water, it tends to stay on the water's surface. As the *Exxon Valdez* spill shows, winds and currents help make the oil spread more quickly, and farther, than in a spill on land.

Working in the Cold and Rain

Whatever it takes to control and clean up a spill, it's up to oil spill cleaners to do the job. They may face subzero temperatures. They may work in blinding rainstorms. They may have to enter icy rivers.

The work is messy. Oil sticks to everything. In a spill on water, the oil spreads on the top of the water in a thin layer called an oil slick. Some of the oil may turn into a substance that looks something like pudding. Oil spill cleaners call this substance "chocolate mousse." The oil can also form small crusty "tar balls." Oil is smelly too. One cleaner described the smell as "worse than rotting meat."

Chocolate Mousse and Tar Balls

Some of the messiest parts of oil spills on water are "chocolate mousse" and "tar balls." Real chocolate mousse is a creamy dessert. The sticky stuff that oil spill cleaners call chocolate mousse is nothing like it. The mousse forms when oil mixes with water. Wind and waves may break up the chocolate mousse into pieces. These can turn into tar balls, hard and crusty on the outside and sticky on the inside.

A long tube called a boom is sometimes used to help control oil spills on water.

Oil-Cleaning Tools

One of the first tasks of cleanup workers at a large spill is to stop the oil from spreading. For a spill on water, they may put long tubes, called **booms**, around the oil. On land, workers may build dirt barriers, known as berms, to block the oil. Sometimes the workers dig trenches to keep the oil from spreading.

Next, workers start cleaning up. They collect as much oil as they can. They skim oil from water using devices called **skimmers**. On shore, workers may use hoses to suck up the oil or flush it away. They also use **super suckers**, powerful vacuums that can suck up the tarlike **sludge**. Sometimes a portion of the collected oil can be recycled for use.

Cleanup workers may also use chemicals to break up the oil. In some cases, they may even set fire to the oil. Both of these methods can cause problems. The chemicals may pollute the environment. Fire produces smoke, and the smoke may harm people and wildlife. When safety precautions are taken, however, these methods can help to quickly deal with some serious spills.

Dangerous Work

Workers clean up an oil spill in Alaska in frigid November weather.

The priority at any oil spill site is safety. Because oil can be dangerous if it touches the skin or if oil fumes are breathed in, oil spill cleaners have to wear special protective gear.

Safety First

Cleanup workers wear what is called personal protective equipment (PPE). This equipment prevents oil from coming into contact with skin or lungs. The gear used can vary. The items worn depend on the size and nature of the spill and the type of oil involved. Good protection in a serious spill can be provided by the following items:

- **Coveralls:** The coveralls are often made of a light plastic material such as Tyvek, which can keep oil from passing through it to the skin.

- **A double layer of gloves:** The double layer provides extra protection. It also lets the oil spill cleaner undress safely. At the end of the day, coveralls and outer gloves may be covered with oil. The worker can use the outer gloves to remove the coveralls, then use the inner gloves to continue to undress.
- **A respirator:** This masklike breathing device can keep a worker from breathing in oil fumes.
- **Eye protection:** Safety glasses protect the eyes from contact with oil or oil fumes.
- **Head protection:** A hard hat can protect the head if the oil spill cleaner is hit by something falling from above.
- **Personal flotation devices (PFDs):** For spills in water, workers in boats and on shore often wear PFDs. The life jackets people wear in rowboats, sailboats, or canoes are examples of PFDs.
- **Steel-toed boots, covered in booties made of a material such as Tyvek:** The boots can keep the feet from being crushed. The booties protect the feet from oil and from other hazards.

Sometimes, oil spill cleaners have to wear a full set of protective gear.

Tyvek

Tyvek is a strong but paper-thin material invented by the DuPont company. It comes in different types. The type used for protective coveralls for oil cleanup workers is usually yellow. It keeps out water and other liquids. It lets water vapor pass through, however. This helps keep the cleanup worker from getting too hot inside the protective suit.

Tyvek isn't used only for protective suits at chemical disaster sites. Another form of Tyvek is used as a "house wrap." Usually white, it provides insulation and protects houses from water damage. The protective covers of CDs and DVDs are made of white Tyvek as well.

Hazardous Conditions

Cleanup workers face danger not only from oil but from the environment. The conditions they work in can be harsh. Surfaces can be slippery. Waterways may be cold and icy. Oil spill cleaners have sometimes even had to remove ice from a river to get at the oil underneath. Cleanup workers have to be on the lookout for animals. During the *Exxon Valdez* spill, workers had to watch out for bears in the cleanup area. In other parts of the world, different animals, such as snakes, might be the chief hazard.

Animals at Risk

Contact with spilled oil can be dangerous to the animals themselves. If they do not get help, they may suffer terrible deaths. Also, they are part of a **food chain**, in which one type, or **species**, of animal feeds on another. The oil can quickly spread from animal to animal as they eat.

Certain animals, such as birds, are especially likely to be harmed. If oil coats the feathers of birds, their wings can become so heavy that they can't fly. Also, the oil causes them to lose their natural waterproofing, and the birds may freeze to death. Oil-coated birds face other threats. Birds tend to clean themselves with their beaks. But when birds with oil-coated feathers do this, the poisonous oil can get into their bodies. Oil also gets into their bodies when they eat fish that have been poisoned by it. In addition, oil affects a bird's **buoyancy**, or ability to float. To keep from sinking, oil-coated birds have to swim extra hard. The birds often die of exhaustion.

Saving Otters

Otters, found in many parts of the world, are also at very high risk from oil spills. They rely on two layers of fur to keep them warm. Oil mats the fur together. This may cause the otters to freeze to death. The oil also makes their fur less buoyant. Then the otters may drown.

In order to save their lives, the animals have to

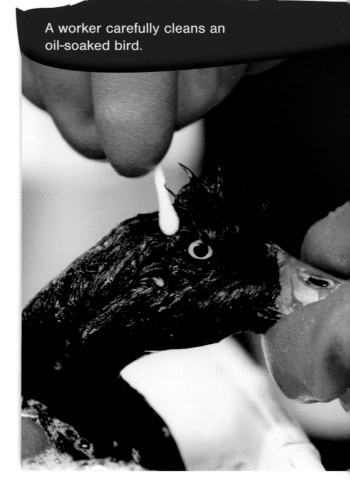

A worker carefully cleans an oil-soaked bird.

Saving the Birds

The best way to keep birds from harm is to keep them away from the oil. Cleanup workers use a method called **hazing** to do this. Hazing involves scaring the birds away with noisemakers, such as horns, or with flashing lights.

When birds do come in contact with oil, workers try to capture them as soon as possible. The birds are given food and water. They are also checked for injuries, such as broken wings.

Birds that are coated with oil are given medication. The medication stops the oil from entering their bloodstream. Workers also wash the birds over and over again. When the birds are healthy and their habitat is safe, they are put back into the wild. They are often tagged so that rescue workers can keep track of them to see if they have really recovered.

be captured. This is not easy. Sea otters, for instance, are usually harmless. When frightened, though, they fight back. A sea otter may weigh 30 pounds (14 kilograms) or more, and it has sharp claws and teeth. Rescue workers may be scratched or bitten. To avoid being bitten, workers put a stick in the otter's mouth. The animal clamps down on it. Many workers still suffer bites and other injuries.

Saving otters sometimes involves placing an oxygen mask over their faces so they can breathe. Oil that the otters may have swallowed is a big worry. Rescuers may feed the animals warmed charcoal. This can help make the oil pass through the body without being absorbed. The otters are given liquid food through a feeding tube. In order to raise their temperature to normal, the otters are put in warm water. Then they are thoroughly washed. Liquid detergent works best. Finally, the otters are dried with blow dryers.

The goal is to return healthy animals to their habitat. Rescuers' efforts don't always work, however. Many animals helped by rescue workers die anyway. The oil can also mean death for many animals that are difficult or impossible for rescue workers to help. These include fish, shellfish, and whales.

Penguin Rescue

An oil spill off the coast of South Africa could have been a tragedy. On June 23, 2000, the ship *Treasure* sank, releasing fuel oil. The oil threatened the world's largest colony of African penguins. This species, sometimes called the black-footed penguin, is found only along the southern African coast. Saving the threatened birds was urgent.

A team that included people from the International Bird Rescue Research Center in California came to the rescue. The first task was to remove as many birds as possible before the oil got to them. To deal with more than 20,000 penguins that were covered in oil, an empty train warehouse was turned into a huge rescue center. Within just a few months, more than 90 percent of the birds were released. They showed no effects of the spill. Because of the rescue effort, a whole species of penguins may have been saved.

Oil on a bird's feathers can make it hard for the bird to keep warm. A sweater was put on one oil-soaked penguin for warmth.

Whatever It Takes

A cleaner uses a towel to help soak up oil from an Alaska beach after the *Exxon Valdez* spill.

Oil spill cleaners make a huge difference. As one worker put it, "We're trying to take care of the environment and return it to its original state as best we can." Whatever it takes, wherever it takes them, oil spill workers do their part to help make the spill site safe and clean.

Every oil spill is different. Oil that is spilled on roadways can end up in trees. The trees or branches then may need to be removed. The oil may seep into sewers. Workers then have to climb into the sewers and scrub them down. This prevents contamination of the water where the sewage system empties. Wherever the oil goes, oil spill workers follow. They have to think on their feet. They need to be able to handle the unexpected.

On Call 24/7

Cleanup work is hard. Workers are on call 24 hours a day, 7 days a week, even on holidays. When spills occur, workers leave their families at a moment's notice. They may have to move to the site of the spill. The living conditions can be rough. Workers may have to live in trailers or on boats for several weeks or months. The *Exxon Valdez* spill workers did so for as long as a year.

The days are long. An average workday on a major spill is 12 hours. Sometimes cleaners may work 40 hours straight. The work—digging, dumping, hauling, and scrubbing—is physically difficult.

Cleaners rest after a long day's work on the *Exxon Valdez* spill.

Much of it is done by hand. Workers scrub rocks with towels or cotton pads. They sweep beaches with special tools called **snares**. They gather garbage that is covered by oil. Many of the tasks are repeated over and over until the area is clean.

Spills and Daily Life

Most oil spills are smaller than the ones that make the news. A small spill may occur, for instance, when a truck or train carrying oil has an accident. Such a spill affects the people who live in the area. Roads may be slippery and impassable for days. If the water supply is affected, people in the neighborhood may need to use bottled water. Such "minor" spills don't only cause problems for people. It is almost certain that plant and animal life will suffer in some way.

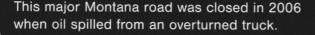

This major Montana road was closed in 2006 when oil spilled from an overturned truck.

Goo Is Everywhere!

"Dirty, nasty, sticky, and sweaty"—that's how oil spill cleaner Tyler Pennington describes his daily work. "The oil turns to goo, especially after it's been in the water before it reaches the beaches. Everything in sight is covered in black goo—including you, if you are doing the cleaning." The job is tedious: "Day after day is spent cleaning the goo off rocks. It seems like it will never end." At the same time, Pennington says, you know that you are "saving the environment, saving the animals, and making sure people are safe. The rewards are worth it."

The Rewards

For oil spill cleaners, the rewards are many. Cleaners work together as a team. All team members have the same goal—to do their best to make everything as clean as it was before the spill. Though it may take a long time, team members often see results.

Alex Davie worked on an oil spill in Puerto Rico. He spoke of the rewards: "When the spill happened, the tropical fish in the tidal pools left. Every day, we watched as more and more fish and sea life returned." The results of his hard work appeared right before his eyes.

Oil in a Swimming Pool?

Sometimes, oil spill cleaners have to use whatever is close at hand. This was the case when an oil barge went aground just off a beach at San Juan, Puerto Rico, in 1994. Oil washed up along the shore. Workers had to find a way to get the oil out of the sand. They took over several swimming pools. "We pumped the sand-oil-tar ball mixture into the pools," the **site commander** said. "Then we stirred up the water until the oil separated out." They removed the sand from the pools, cleaned the sand, and then returned it to the beaches.

Becoming an Oil Spill Cleaner

A California cleanup crew washes rocks affected by a 2007 oil spill.

Oil spill cleanup has been called a "thinking person's job." The work is physical, but oil spill cleaners need to think on their feet. They need to be able to react quickly. They need to communicate well.

Oil spill cleaners also need to be good at working as a team. At major spills the team is usually headed by a site commander. The site commander oversees the cleanup. Next, supervisors direct the cleanup workers. Finally, there are the cleaners themselves. Working as a team, they handle the messy hands-on work of the cleanup.

Oil Spill Training

In the United States, oil spill workers in most cases must have a high school diploma. Workers usually learn how to do the job in two ways. The first is to take a training class that meets standards set by the U.S. government. Two agencies set these standards—the Occupational Safety and Health Administration and the Environmental Protection Agency (EPA). The training class must be taken before someone can get a job as a member of a cleanup team. The second way oil spill cleaners learn is on the job. There,

Specialist Workers

Different kinds of specialists may take part in cleaning up major spills. A health and safety officer deals with health risks. He or she may have a college degree in a field such as environmental science. Geologists, chemists, and other scientists take water and soil samples. They study the samples to help figure out the type and extent of damage that has been caused by the oil spill. Veterinarians (doctors who treat animals) and other animal health experts may also work at a spill site.

they are trained about equipment, safety issues, and what to expect at an oil spill site.

Disaster Drill

It takes practice to become a good oil spill cleaner. By practicing, workers can figure out what works and what doesn't. They can apply what they learn to a real spill. A center called Ohmsett in New Jersey serves as the national oil spill response test facility. It has a tank holding 2.6 million gallons (9.8 million liters) of water. Here, using real equipment, people practice how to cope with spills under various conditions.

Real oil is used in the Ohmsett tank. But spill cleanup practice elsewhere usually has to be done without real oil. For practicing some skills, computer programs can be used to prepare workers for dealing with a spill. For a spill on water, for instance, the programs determine which way the oil will flow based on tides, wind, and ocean currents. They may create images to make the drill seem more real. Workers also practice on-site. When drills take place in the water and along shorelines, colored dye or a substance like peat moss might be used as oil, and oranges in place of "tar balls." Using booms and skimmers, workers clean up the mess just as they would oil.

The dye put into the water by this ship takes the place of oil in a spill-cleanup drill.

Who Hires Oil Spill Cleaners?

Oil spill cleaners usually work for a company or for a government agency. Their job may require them to do more than just oil cleanup tasks. These other duties will depend on what the organization they work for does.

One Million Cleaners

It was the worst oil spill in the history of South Korea. On December 8, 2007, a barge rammed into the tanker *Hebei Spirit* off the country's western coast. About 3 million gallons (11 million liters) of oil spilled out of the ship. More than 100 miles (160 kilometers) of coast were affected. The area around the county of Taean was especially hard-hit. The cleanup was aided by more than one million volunteers who rushed to help out. "The efforts of the volunteers have truly created a miracle in Taean," said one official.

Large numbers of South Koreans helped clean up oil spilled in a 2007 ship crash.

In the United States, two federal organizations oversee the cleanup of large spills. If a spill occurs in a coastal area or around the Mississippi River, the Coast Guard is in charge. For spills in inland areas, the EPA is generally in charge. The Coast Guard has a "strike" team to deal with oil spills. The EPA also has a staff of oil spill experts.

The actual cleanup work may be carried out by the company considered responsible for the spill. For this reason, oil companies often have their own cleanup teams. There also are environmental companies that do cleanup work. They have crews and equipment that can be sent out to oil spill sites. Environmental companies may be hired by the company responsible for a spill, or they may be hired by the government.

Fire departments are another place where cleaners may find jobs. Some fire departments have hazardous materials ("hazmat") teams that deal with local spills caused by tanker trucks or trains. These specialists are usually the first to respond to a spill. They are generally trained in a variety of hazardous waste cleanup methods.

The Role of Volunteers

Volunteers can sometimes do important work. These are people who don't belong to an official cleanup crew but are willing to help out, without pay. Still, it is important to remember that cleanup requires special efforts. Volunteers need to know how to be safe around animals and birds and around the oil itself.

There are many places where volunteers can get training. Among the organizations offering training sessions are the Coast Guard, government environmental agencies,

Firefighters in Kenya, Africa, try to put out burning oil from a crashed oil truck.

Bird Rescuers

Since it was started in 1971, the International Bird Rescue Research Center has helped save birds at more than 200 oil spill sites in the United States and around the world.

state fish and game offices, and some fire departments. Other good sources of training include groups such as the International Bird Rescue Research Center in California. This organization has been active in the rescue of birds all over the world. It has helped

So You Want to Be an Oil Spill Cleaner

To become an oil spill cleaner, people have to pass a special training class. In addition, workers have to take a refresher course every year. Training is not all that's needed. Steve Ohrwaschel, corporate vice president of the company Lewis Environmental, puts it this way: "Workers have to be mentally tough and physically tough." Most of all, according to Ohrwaschel, workers have to be willing to change their lifestyle. Being on call 24 hours a day and working many hours of overtime aren't easy. But oil spill workers take a special pride in the help they provide when disaster strikes.

out at spills in such places as Alaska, South Africa, and California's San Francisco Bay. It provides training and instructional programs to make sure that volunteers are as effective as possible.

Being a volunteer can be a good way for people to learn if oil spill cleanup is something they would really want to do as a career.

Filling a Need

Oil spill cleaners have to meet many requirements. They must be good at working outdoors, especially in water. They must be willing to do physical labor. They must take direction well and be able to live away from home for long periods of time. They have to be comfortable getting messy, getting wet, and solving problems.

Most of all, oil spill cleaners must care about people. They must also have respect for animals. And they must believe in preserving the environment. As long as people need oil—and as long as the environment is in danger—the world will need hardworking, courageous oil spill cleaners.

barge: A large flat-bottom boat that carries oil or other cargo. Barges are often used in rivers and canals.

blowout: A sudden release of oil caused by the buildup of pressure in an oil well.

boom: A long tube used to prevent oil spills on water from spreading.

buoyancy: The ability to float.

fertilizer: A substance containing chemicals that can help living things (such as plants) grow.

food chain: A series of living things that depend on each other for food. Each member of the series uses the next member as a food source.

habitat: The place where an animal or a plant normally lives.

hazing: The practice of scaring birds away using loud sounds or lights.

microbe: A very tiny living thing. Microbes usually can be seen only through a microscope.

reef: An underwater ridge of rock, sand, or coral that is close to the surface of the water.

site commander: The person in charge of an oil spill cleanup site.

skimmer: A device used to skim oil off the surface of water.

sludge: A semisolid material that forms as oil and water mix.

snare: A device used for sweeping oil off beaches. It has long strips of material that can absorb oil and looks something like a pom-pom.

species: A group of living things that have the same makeup and characteristics and can breed with one other.

super sucker: A high-powered vacuum used to clean up spilled oil.

tanker: A large ship that carries liquid cargo, such as oil.

BOOKS

Beech, Linda Ward. *The Exxon Valdez's Deadly Oil Spill*. New York: Bearport, 2007.

Dils, Tracey. *The Exxon Valdez*. Philadelphia: Chelsea House, 2001.

Owens, Peter. *Man-Made Disasters: Oil and Chemical Spills*. San Diego, CA: Lucent, 2003.

Parks, Peggy J. *Oil Spill*. Detroit: KidHaven Press, 2005.

WEBSITES

http://www.cleangulfassoc.com
This website is from Clean Gulf Associates, a group focusing on the Gulf of Mexico. It shows many examples of equipment used in cleaning up oil spills.

http://www.Ohmsett.com
This website of the National Oil Spill Response Test Tank Facility includes information about oil spills and cleanup, along with videos showing the use of some cleanup techniques.

http://www.oilspillinfo.org
This website from the American Petroleum Institute tells about the prevention and cleanup of oil spills and includes a large history section.

http://oils.gpa.unep.org/kids/kids.htm
This website sponsored by the United Nations Environment Program provides many links to good information about oil and pollution.

http://response.restoration.noaa.gov
The Students and Teachers section of this website from the U.S. National Oceanic and Atmospheric Administration contains a great deal of information about oil spills.

http://uscg.mil/hq/nsfweb
This is the website of the branch of the U.S. Coast Guard that responds to spills of oil and other dangerous substances.

 **INDEX**

About the Author Tracey E. Dils is the author of more than 40 books for children. She received the Parents' Choice Award for *A Young Author's Guide to Publishers* and the Ohioana Award for Children's Literature.

For help with research on this book, the author especially thanks oil spill professionals Alex Davie, Tyler Pennington, Steve Ohrwaschel, Mark Malvern, John Gustafson, Bill Greeneisen, and U.S. Coast Guard Petty Officer First Class Neil Gibb.